To:
Ryan + Becca

Thanks + Merry christmas

Karen Moore
12/25/2011

Acknowledgments

Special thanks to Jack Potter, Patsi Morton, Gladys Shay, Brian Kennedy, Lanny Luding and Tom Ulrich for all their help.

Front cover: Grizzly bear in evening light, Many Glacier. Chris Peterson photo.

At right: Going-to-the-Sun Mountain reflects in St. Mary Lake, Glacier National Park. Mel Ruder photo.

Back cover: Gunsight Pass, 1947, Mel Ruder photo.

Edited and designed by Chris Peterson

Brian Kennedy photos © Brian Kennedy Tom Ulrich photos © Tom Ulrich Chris Peterson photos © Chris Peterson Mel Ruder photos © Hungry Horse News, with the exception of Ruder bear photos, which are © Mel Ruder. Bear on picnic table is © Hungry Horse News/Mel Ruder.

A portion of the proceeds from this book benefit the Glacier Natural History Association.

ISBN 0-9768946-0-2 © Hungry Horse News

Created in Columbia Falls, Montana

Printed in Hong Kong

Glacier
at a Gallop

Mel Ruder, the man who started it al

Mel Ruder came to Columbia Falls in July, 1946, to start a newspaper. He was 31 years old. Mel had egg on his tie when he came to the home of my aunt and uncle, John and Claudia O'Connell one Sunday morning. He offered me a job, I accepted and moved to Columbia Falls and became first employee Aug. 1, 1946. First edition was printed Aug. 8, 1946.

Chris Raaen owned a building on Nucleus Avenue which was rented by the State Liquor Store and Bill Nadeau's radio shop. Chris divided the building and the north half became the first *Hungry Horse News* office.

A *Spokesman Review* reporter/photographer was doing a special about Hungry Horse Dam. He came to the newspaper office to interview Mel and wanted me to pose on the corner of his desk. Mel was upset because he did not want readers to think I always sat there. Chris stood on a ladder in front of the window, holding the *Hungry Horse News* sign for the picture. It had not been attached to the building.

Glacier Cafe was across from the newspaper office on Nucleus Avenue. Most days his only meal was a hamburger and milkshake. He developed film using a drawer in the chest of drawers. There were frequent power outages. Mel always kept a candle on his desk for working nights. It was good we did not have electric typewriters.

The newspaper office was home for the Columbia Falls branch of the Flathead County Library. Mel received $15 month salary as librarian. This was about the time Mel advertised that cats could be left at the office if owners wanted to find a new home for their pets. He started his policy of not charging for classads if a person was advertising for employment. The *News* moved into its new building — a log cabin on what then was Highway 40 — in December 1947. The offices are still there today.

Mel was employed as a photographer by Haynes in Yellowstone National Park during the 1930s. His name was on the masthead of a park publication printed years later, but credit lines for individual photos were not given.

Weekly trips by Mel included Glacier National Park, Hungry Horse Dam, new communities of Hungry Horse, Martin City, Hungry Horse Village, South Fork Town, which he called the Beerless Boom Town, and longtime communities of Coram, Belton (now West Glacier) Lake McDonald, and other areas. Photos ranged from cutting ice on Lake Five to Easter pictures of boys and girls with new lambs in Bad Rock.

We knew where Mel had traveled when photos were printed.

The magnificent photos of Glacier National Park were responsible for continuing subscriptions received from readers throughout the world. Mel knew names of the peaks, locations, hiked the trails lugging his heavy camera, and captured it all on film. He had patience photographing park animals which was lacking when taking pictures of humans. Sometimes beauties of the park were overshadowed by tragedies. Mel would be there with camera, notebook and pencil, whether it was a mauling by a bear or lost hikers or climbers. One I remember vividly is when park crews were caught in an avalanche. Mel covered the catastrophe and longtime friend, Jean Sullivan, was one of the men rescued.

Mel's photo of a grinning Dr. W. F. Bennett, Columbia Falls physician, standing beside a happy Jean Sullivan was a classic.

Mel became Chamber of Commerce president and secretary. He joined Columbia Falls Lodge No. 89, AF&AM, and was proud when he became a director of the Bank of Columbia Falls. He liked to tell about being an Eagle Scout in North Dakota.

Mel grieved when he reported tragedies or wrote obituaries of friends. Some acquaintances felt his last name was synonymous with Mel's personality. Those who knew him

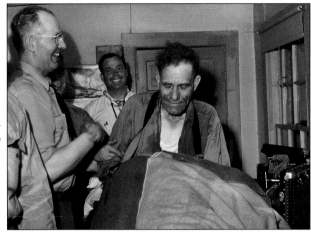

Road crewman Jean Sullivan survived an avalanche that buried him for hours on the Sun Highway in May, 1953 while he was setting explosives. Here he is with Dr. W.F. Bennett and M.E. Beatty recovering on a table in the mess hall at Road Camp. The slide killed co-workers Blackie Beaton and Bill Whitford. Ruder covered the million-acre Park like no other journalist.

well were aware of his sensitive side and situations when helped others without publicity. He did demand thank y notes.

Mel began the Columbia Falls Children's Fund when young girl in Columbia Falls was badly burned.

Mel knew financial assistance was required with transportation and medical costs and started the fund. It still exists. He also started the Memorial Foundation for Montana Veterans Home. Monetary gifts given to the Foundation are used to finance special projects not finan by the state.

Community correspondents wrote their local news for *Hungry Horse News.* These included rural areas around Columbia Falls and the Canyon. They were not paid and added a lot to the paper. Mel would leave out advertising rather than stories. Business owners were not always plea

Mel was frugal. Natural gas thermostats were all for minimum heat and lowest watt lightbulbs were used the shop. He bought lunch for printers, a plain hamburg on press days.

We did make one pot of coffee daily for the office. The was not a retirement plan for employees.

Mel had a sixth sense for news, was dogmatic, and a perfectionist. He would becom very irritated if a story had a release date after the *Hungry Horse News* went to press. H was utterly disgusted if a prominent citizen died after press day and a daily had the sto first. We did not have scanners and computers so it took a lot of telephone calls to get details.

I often wondered what customers thought when they walked into the newspaper o Mel typed with only two fingers and was alternately chewing his fingernails or twistin hair as he concentrated.

We would both be muttering to ourselves as we wrote and more than one person thought we were speaking to each other.

Mel insisted he was the only person to take pictures for the *Hungry Horse News.* W had almost hurricane-force winds once when Mel was out of town. Trees were uproote and the Louisiana Pacific office building picked up and turned slightly on the foundati was assistant editor in charge during Mel's absences.

Ralph Ammondson, printer, went with me and he took pictures and I wrote stories about damage ranging from the Red Bridge area to west of Columbia Falls.

Mel did not complain when he saw the newspaper. Mel was a school board membe when Ruth Bergan was hired as a Columbia Falls High School English teacher. Whe they were married Mel drove off and left Ruth's suitcase on the lawn. We had to send them.

Mel's work was not finished when the paper went to press. He would deliver the ca sales to stores in Columbia Falls, up the Canyon, to Whitefish and Kalispell. He also t mail bags to post offices. It was a sad day for postal crews if papers were not in subscri post offices or rural mail boxes Friday mornings.

In later years Mel and Ruth enjoyed traveling. His Bystander column was used to tell trip highlights and of course there were photos.

When I telephoned Mel to inform him that he had won the Pulitzer Prize he exclai "now I can die!" I am glad he waited many years. After all, the *Hungry Horse News* was Mel's life. Mel passed away Nov. 19, 2000.

— *Gladys (Van)*

Park Superintendent Keith Neilson and Dawn Mist Falls, on a summer trip from Many Glacier to Waterton, 1966.

L.O. Vaught spent 50 summers in Glacier and wrote about the Park's early history. He first came to Glacier in 1898. A mountain overlooking Lake McDonald is named after him. Here he is photographed August 15, 1953.

By the summer of 1947, just a year after its founding, Ruder began running photo spreads of Glacier on the front page. This photo was taken in July of Mount Brown fire lookouts Doyle and Carol Kincaid. Headline on the front page read 'Fire Ranks as Biggest Threat to Glacier.' Today the lookout is still on Mount Brown, just below summit, though it is no longer manned on a regular basis. Glacier now lets some wild-fires burn, depending on their location and threats to humans and structures.

'In this land where we live, pictures are like Christmas card scenes,' Ruder writes in a Christmas photo spread in 1950. Here, Ranger Roy Hutchinson looks at Glacier Mount Stimson, elevation 10,142 feet. It was a fairly dry winter, Ruder remarked. There was only about 20 inches of snow on the ground. The year before there had been 4

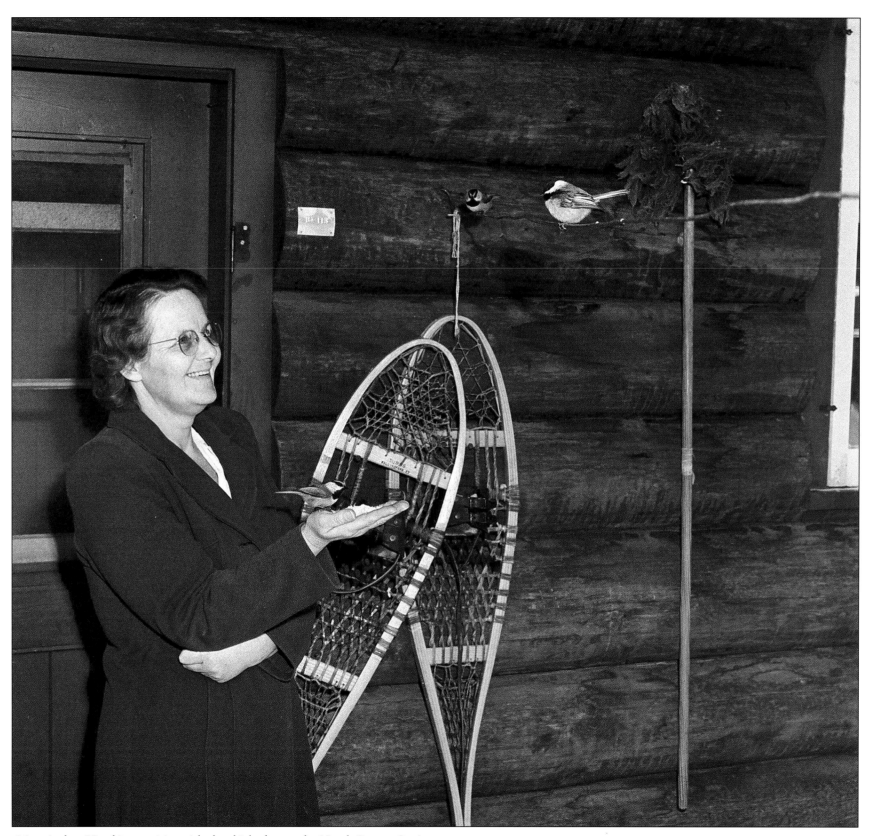

Mrs. Audrey Hutchinson visits with the chickadees at the Nyack Ranger Station.

Horses and Glacier: The Perfect Fit

Ruder often went on Park horseback expeditions in Glacier. This shot was from an August 1959 trip to Fifty Mountain, a remote camp in Glacier along the Continental Divide. On the trip were District Ranger Ralph Shaver, trail foreman Bill Yenne, Abel Bergan, who worked in the Park in the 1920s and '30s, Harvey Reynolds, who used to work in Yellowstone and Irvin Lloyd, Glacier's landscape architect.

It was 18 miles from Packer's Roost and then 12 miles down to Mineral Creek back to the Sun Road.

They spent the night at Fifty Mountain. The dicey part of the trip was crossing the steep snowfield near Ahern Pass by horse. A slip could mean the end of you and your horse. The negatives are marked as taken in August, but the spread published on September 4, 1959.

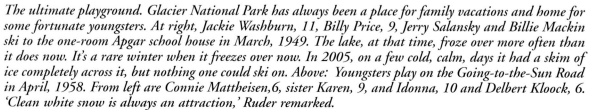

The ultimate playground. Glacier National Park has always been a place for family vacations and home for some fortunate youngsters. At right, Jackie Washburn, 11, Billy Price, 9, Jerry Salansky and Billie Mackin ski to the one-room Apgar school house in March, 1949. The lake, at that time, froze over more often than it does now. It's a rare winter when it freezes over now. In 2005, on a few cold, calm, days it had a skim of ice completely across it, but nothing one could ski on. Above: Youngsters play on the Going-to-the-Sun Road in April, 1958. From left are Connie Mattheisen, 6, sister Karen, 9, and Idonna, 10 and Delbert Kloock, 6. 'Clean white snow is always an attraction,' Ruder remarked.

Miss Glacier National Park 1963 was Nicki Smith, 'a 19-year-old vocalist and chambermaid.' Smith was crowned by Don Hummel, the president of Glacier Park Inc. Smith was from Moses Lake, Wash. Today, you'll see more women in greens or jeans than dresses in the Park.

uder titled this negative 'Cheesecake and Garden Wall.' But in print, the photo caption said, 'Joanne Johnson St. Olaf College co-ed who works at Glacier Park Lodge, elped this photo of the Garden Wall. She wet her toe in a mountain stream that flowed from a snowbank 40 feet from the road.' The Garden Wall marks the Continental Divide north of Logan Pass.

A Favorite Vista

Horses have long been used in Glacier National Park and most trails are cut to accommodate them. Here, assistant Chief Ranger Dick Nelson and steed Red Eagle, 1947. This view looks back toward Mt. Siyeh, Going-to-the-Sun Mountain, and Citadel. Ruder remarked that this was taken on an Indian summer day. 'H.H. News isn't ready to take snow pictures.'

Portrait of old-time packer Jay Lytle, photographed in August, 1956. At right, Packer Ron Sherman along with carpenters Eugene Lance and Lee Yorton pack a new roof up to Swiftcurrent Lookout. The lookout, at elevation 8,436, is perched above Granite Park Chalet. The photo was part of a spread on 'Mules Take Roof Up Mountain.' Tagging along, the story said, was the Hungry Horse News editor. Fanny, a large mule, carried the roof. 'A mule carrying a roof is something to see.' In the winter, Sherman drove a taxi cab in Reno, Nev. In the summer, he packed in supplies to Glacier's lookouts and to remote trail crews. Packers are still used extensively today to bring in supplies to the park's chalets and other remote locations.

17

Glacier National Park packer Stu Sorensen en route to Swiftcurrent Lookout in July, 1976. Heaven's Peak is in the background. Today, Sorensen works for the Montana Department of Transportation, but he still rides his mules in 0-Mok-Sees, which is Blackfeet for 'games on horseback.'

Park naturalist David Casteel points out mountain goats on the cliffs above Iceberg Lake in July, 1973. The park still offers guided hikes and Iceberg Lake is just as popular now as it was then. The lake doesn't contain true icebergs, but large chunks of ice that break up as summer progresses. A swim in this lake is almost unbearably cold.

Glacier at the Movies

There have been plenty of movies shot in Glacier over the years. At right are Ronald Reagan and Barbara Stanwyck in the 'Cattle Queen of Montana,' shot in the St. Mary Valley in July 1954. Remarked Ruder: The story isn't based on history, but combined with good scenery, name stars and an action plot, it should make a very credible western. Modern-day reviews give it a 4.6 out of 10, though it does get a plus for, you guessed it, Glacier's fantastic scenery.

In this scene from *Cattle Queen*, Reagan plants two kegs of gunpowder under a wagon. Reagan played a hired gun named Farrell, who abandons his employer and comes to the aid of Stanwyck's character. The film was shot in Technicolor and the wagon was actually blown up.

October, 1959 transformed the Going-to-the-Sun Road into the Korean War movie 'All the Young Men,' starring Sidney Poitier, then heavyweight champion Ingemar Johansson and Alan Ladd. Blackfeet Indians played the role of Koreans in the film. Like a lot films made in Glacier, it received mixed reviews. In the film, Poitier leads an all-white battalion against the Chinese. Here, the troops march up the Going-to-the-Sun Road near Logan Pass. In the background is Going-to-the-Sun Mountain.

n explosion rocks the troops as the Korean War is fought at Logan Pass during the filming of 'All the Young Men.' In an accompanying story, Ruder remarked that the fil-
akers welcomed the snow, but needed the sun to finish shooting. Sun came and this shot was made on Saturday, Oct. 17, 1959.

One of Hollywood's greatest flops of all time was filmed in Glacier in 1979. Here, Two Medicine is transformed into an 1890s old west town for Michael Cimino's 'Heaven's G[...] This photo has never been published. The buildings, with the exception of the church, were built on scene. The movie was a critical and box office disaster however. The best t[...] about it might be this view, with Mount Sinopah rising in the background. Then Superintendent Phil Iversen eventually banned further filming of Heaven's Gate in Glacier, [...] problems with this set. Cimino wanted to film more scenes in the North Fork.

'Garden Wall Devastated by Fire,' the headline read on Sept. 8, 1967. Here, Washington correspondent Maarten C. Bolle of the Netherlands and a woman, who is not identified, watch the blaze. The photo was taken Sept. 4 1967. The Garden Wall would burn again in spectacular fashion on July 23, 2003 when the Trapper Creek Fire burned to the Loop on the Going-to-the-Sun Road. The 2003 fire ran into the 1967 regeneration, which was mostly soft-wood trees and stopped its expansion almost as if someone had drawn a line in the forest. A photo of the Trapper Creek Fire appears later in this book. This photo wasn't published.

Hold onto your hats, men

Two Medicine is famous for its wind. Here Park Superintendent Bill Briggle and Lewis Gannaway, trail maintenance supervisor, hold their hats while on a trip from Two Medicine to Ole Creek. In the background is administrative officer Al Schwarz. The trio stopped for a photo at Two Medicine Pass. It was a three-day excursion through the heart of Glacier's southern region. Ruder remarked that wind gusts hit 60 mph at Firebrand Pass, which is near Marias Pass.

Glacier, the classroom

July, 1951, at 10 a.m. and at 2 p.m., Ruder writes, the park offers naturalist hikes from Logan Pass to Hidden Lake Overlook. Park Naturalist Art Noskowiak gives a tour in this classic view. The Garden Wall stretches out behind the group. The overlook is reached 'in just 40 minutes,' Ruder writes.

Belton-Apgar and Martin City Cub Scouts were overnight campers at Bowman Lake in October, 1948. In above photo, Tom Harrington watches a deer swim the lake. Today, Bowman is still a very popular camping spot for visitors. The campground still has a healthy population of resident deer as well.

July 9, 1965, naturalist A.M. Johnson guides a group to St. Mary Falls. The falls today is still one of Glacier's most popular hikes. This photo was not published, but the photo on the next page was. In the same issue, Ruder admonishes retail giant Sears Roebuck for an ad it produced of a phone booth superimposed at the Wild Goose Island Overlook. 'Glacier isn't about to erect a phone booth at such a location.'

Naturalist A.M. Johnson with group at St. Mary Lake. 'Glacier is the nation's foremost trail park,' Ruder remarked. It has more than 700 miles of trails. You can spend a lifetime hiking there and still miss entire regions.

May 23, 1969, Naturalist John Tyers and Columbia Falls seventh-graders. Today students from across Flathead and Glacier County still attend park-led field trips.

...w line for visitors at Glacier's open house commemorating its 50th anniversary on May 10, 1960 at Avalanche Campground. In this group were Supervisor and Mrs. F.J. ...zling of the Flathead National Forest, Mr. and Mrs. Gordon Rognlien, Flathead County Commissioners Henry Irwin, Harley Houston and Oscar Wendt and Glenn E. ...house, County Clerk. Chef was Ranger Jim Thompson. Ruder didn't always identify women by their first name, particularly if they were married.

'Logan Pass had

winter look on top Sunday, but it was too warm to wear a jacket in bright sun.' (Ruder often left out articles in his writing. It saved space.) New snow saw skiers. Average closing date is Oct. 22. This photo was taken October 4, 1969. The photo wasn't published, though the skier has that '60s look. The mountain in the background is Clements.

Winter companions
a no-no in today's Park

But in March, 1949, Miles Stromen and his wife were the only winter-time residents in upper McDonald region of Glacier. Here, Stromen feeds a deer they named Lippy a piece of bread. Feeding animals in Glacier today will get you a hefty fine.

In a typical winter Glacier can see hundreds of inches of snow. The weight, as one might guess, can be detrimental to a cabin's roof. Here, John Fabian and son Lynn shovel snow off a cabin roof at Lake McDonald. Fabian lived in the log home all winter with his family. Today, caretakers still live next to Lake McDonald Lodge through the winter months.

Plowing the Going-to-the-Sun Road is dangerous business. No one knows that better than Chuck Siderius, whose bulldozer in June 1964 plummeted off the edge of the road some 350 vertical feet after a slab of snow gave way. Siderius somehow survived the tumble. Here, crews bring the dozer back up to the highway and once uprighted, it was back plowing the road again. The accident happened off the Big Drift, an area of the road that sees 100 feet of snow in many years.

We were unable to locate the original photo caption of this picture taken on July 4, 1961 at Granite Park Chalet. But according to Lanny Luding, whose family operat the chalets, this is probably Hazel Briggs, of Spokane, Wash., who worked as a baker at the chalet in 1960-61. This is a favorite because of its simplicity. Many of Rude photos had infinite depth of field. This one does not. The building in the background is not the chalet itself, but the living quarters.

Ranger Jerry Banta 'on inspection' along the Sun Highway on Nov. 7, 1969. Snow shuts down the road for good usually in October, though it can snow any month of the year.

The Honeymoon Suite

June honeymooners in Glacier were Don and Barbara Loeffler of St. Paul, Minn. in the Many Glacier Valley. Mountain in the background is Wilbur, which Don climbed the previous summer.

Glacier National Park's icon: An inquisitive mountain goat near Sperry Chalet, Aug. 1977. Problem, Ruder said, was the goat was too close.

Always photogenic, a mountain goat 'poses' on a rock for visiting college students from Minnesota in this August, 1977 photo. Watching are Greg and Ed Peters, Steve Sampair and Briane Milke. Goats are a generally affable and tolerant creature, even with those needle sharp horns.

Learning the ropes

And kick and glide and kick and glide... Park rangers learn the skiing ropes at West Glacier's Lion Hill, in January, 1959. Teaching the class was Chief Ranger H. Gordon Bender. From left to right were Clarence Bengtson, park road maintenance supervisor and rangers Elvin Aaberg, Marvin Hershey, Keith Miller, Bob Morris, and Donald Dayton; and engineers Charles Riebe, Bob Hafferman and John Higgins.

49

A Favorite Valley

The Many Glacier Valley may be the finest in the Rocky Mountain West. It was a Ruder favorite as well. At left, a band of Rocky Mountain Bighorn sheep cross the valley near at the Ranger Station in April, 1964. The photo has a timeless quality — the same photo, on the right day, could be taken today. One has to get up early to get good photos of the east side. The light can be spectacular, particularly in the fall. The problem is the wind. Most days, the wind wants to nudge you off your perch or at least blow your hat away. Below: Dick Nelson and a friend at the National Governor's Conference, June 28, 1960. The photo wasn't published, but Ruder went to some lengths to get others. He took off his shoes, rolled up his pants, and waded out into a pond to get a picture of Canadian Prime Minister John G. Diefenbaker. All in a day's work at the Hungry Horse News.

Some of Glacier's landscapes have changed through the years. Here, Ranger Paul Webb looks at the Two Medicine Chalet. Deemed unsafe and having been unoccupied for years, the chalets were burned down in May, 1956.

'here was a bit of heartache,' Ruder wrote about the destruction of the Two Medicine Chalets. He noted that one of them was reported to be the location of one of President *inklin* Roosevelt's famed 'fireside chats,' in 1934. Today, the Park has put millions into restoring its remaining historic structures, including the Many Glacier Hotel.

Giving thanks

On Thanksgiving Day, 1968, Park Ranger Al Hoover was also on patrol. Ruder went with him and took this shot of Hoover standing on the shores of Bowman Lake. Rising in the background is Rainbow Peak, so named for its many different bands of colored rock.

A Stroll in the Park

Sheep populations in Many Glacier can have great fluctuations, as the animals are prone to disease and the ill effects of a bad winter. Here, sheep researcher Robert Riggs walks along Swiftcurrent Lake while his subjects head the other direction in this Dec. 21, 1975 photo. Looming in the distance is Mount Wilbur, one of Glacier's most rugged, and photographed, peaks.

65

It's rare to see a woman hiking in a dress these days, but other than that, Virginia Falls hasn't changed much in 40 years. The bridge is still wooden and the falls are spectacular — just a mile and a half from the Going-to-the-Sun Road.

'It's comfortable in Glacier,' Ruder remarked. Logan Pass is one of those rare places where people sunbathe on snow. Mr. and Mrs. S.M. Askevold and the Berthelote family of Polson were having a picnic in the background, while a young skier caught some rays. Photo was taken in the early 1950s.

The value of signs ... We were unable to locate the original photo caption, but bear traps haven't changed much over the decades. They still pretty much look like this. They'[re] put on a trailer so once the bear is caught, it can be moved to another location — away from people.

A black bear helps itself to lunch after the picnickers left the table, May 30, 1958 at Avalanche Campground. The bear was hazed off the table by camp tender Henry Schneider shortly after Ruder grabbed this photo. Today, bears still get into human food on occasion, but only because of human carelessness. Garbage receptacles in Glacier are nearly bearproof and warnings are on every picnic table about leaving food. The motto is 'a fed bear is a dead bear,' because once they start getting into human foods, a bear will never stop, eventually getting itself killed.

A Popular Bruin

Whitey was a popular bear along the Going-to-the-Sun Road in 1948. Despite her color, she is a black bear. Black bears in Glacier run from jet black to cinnamon red to blonde to brown. A wet brown black bear will look like a grizzly to folks unfamiliar with bears. Grizzlies have a much rounder profile and a distinctive hump on their back. They also generally have a grumpier disposition. All bears should be treated with respect and caution. Feeding them is a definite no-no.

Feeding bears is taboo, Ruder wrote in July 23, 1961. Reason is bears do not distinguish between food and the hands that feed them. Today bear watching in Glacier is still a favorite activity. Though folks just watch, they don't feed. Park rangers also monitor 'bear jams' closely. A bear jam, as you might guess, is when traffic piles up to view a bruin. Polite folks take a picture or two so the car behind him can take a peek, too.

This bear of the early 1950s was first named Gloomy Gus. Then she had triplets and her name was changed to Gussie.

A climber looks down at Hidden Lake from the airy perch of Mount Cannon in Sept. 1987.

Brian Kennedy

In October 1978 a young Brian Kennedy of Wyoming took the helm as editor of the Hungry Horse News.

He was 23 years old at the time.

Kennedy would carry the photography torch at the Hungry Horse News for the next 20 years.

More than any other Hungry Horse News photographer, Kennedy was a mountain climber. He's climbed all of Glacier's 10,000-foot peaks, plus countless others. Kennedy climbed with the likes of J. Gordon Edwards, the "patron saint" of climbing in Glacier.

Kennedy gave readers views of Glacier that hadn't been seen before. Take his shot of Joe Steffen on page 83 at Mount Wilbur's summit, in August, 1987.

Steffen has his shirt off and is looking back down at Iceberg Lake, thousands of feet below. It's a classic shot that requires one to have more than just photographer in your blood, you need a little mountain goat, too.

Kennedy also brought color to the pages Hungry Horse News in the late 1990s. Now readers didn't have to imagine the brilliance of the fall leaves or the glow of the wildflowers — they saw it in print.

When he hired me in 1998, Kennedy took great pains to teach me to recognize the color in my photos.

I'd show him something I thought was a "whiz-bang for sure" shot for the front page and he'd look at it and say, "Ah, it doesn't have good color."

And on an inside page it went.

If you're going to run color, you'd better celebrate it.

Kennedy sold the paper in January, 1999.

He still lives in Columbia Falls. He still is an active mountain climber with the Glacier Mountaineer Society and one will often see him at local basketball games shooting photos for himself.

He gambled on a young photographer from New York just a few months before he sold the paper. For that roll of the dice, I am forever indebted.

— **Chris Peterson**

cow and calf elk wait out a spring snowstorm in St. Mary in May, 1984.

The kids are all right. Kid mountain goats take a break near Mount Oberlin while their nannies grazed nearby.

The man who wrote the book on climbing in Glacier was J. Gordon Edwards. Here Kennedy took his photo on July 30, 1986 on the goat trail along the Ptarmigan Wall. Edwards book, 'A Climber's Guide to Glacier National Park,' is a Bible for anyone looking to bag one of Glacier's peaks.

Winter Journey

A skier makes her way through the Red Bench burn in March 1989. The Red Bench Fire scorched the park's North Fork region in the summer of 1988, destroying the pole bridge across the North Fork of the Flathead River and nearly burning down the unincorporated town of Polebridge. Today, new trees in the burn are about 15 feet high.

Little Bighorn

In Glacier, the mountains are big. We make sure of that in our photos, Brian Kennedy told me when I first started working for the Hungry Horse News. This is what he meant. Mount Wilbur and a bighorn sheep on what looks to be a fairly pleasant day for November, 1985 in Many Glacier.

Seeing wolf tracks in Glacier would not be a rare thing. The park has anywhere from three to four packs living in its one million-plus acres. But actually seeing a wolf is another story. Glacier's wolves are elusive creatures. Kennedy captured this photo of one near Big Prairie in 1992.

'The mountains are calling, and I must go,' said John Muir. Kennedy was an avid mountain climber throughout his career, lugging a camera along. He still climbs today. Here is fellow climber Joe Steffen on Mount Wilbur's summit, August, 1987. Below is Iceberg Lake.

Then Vice President George H. Bush, center, with Park Superintendent Bob Haraden and Wyoming Senator Alan Simpson at Logan Pass. Glacier's beauty attracts all folks.

Boardwalks aren't just for humans. This grizzly bear was a show-stopper in August of 1986 when it decided to dig up some roots near the Hidden Lake boardwalk. Hundreds of folks stopped to watch while park rangers kept an eye on the crowd, and the bear.

Shangri-La

Glacier has more than 700 miles of trails, but the real Park is often found away from the beaten path. Here, Ray Allen looks over the Many Glacier Valley from Shangri-La, a high basin below Mount Wilbur, home to herds of mountain goats and wildflowers.

Good morning

August 1984, morning light at Granite Park Chalet. Notice the laundry is hung out to dry. Perched above the McDonald Valley, it was built in 1914 by the Great Northern Railroad. Getting there is about a 7.5 mile hike which is fairly level, or by taking the Loop Trail four miles from the Going-to-the-Sun Road with about a half-mile of elevation gain. Every step is worth it.

Perhaps the most photographed spot in Glacier is the Wild Goose Island overlook at St. Mary Lake.

Glacier is a place of secret gardens and waterfalls.

A Sacred Place

Chief Mountain is considered a sacred place by the Blackfeet people. This view is from east of the peak, looking back into the park. The gnarled aspens show their fall colors.

Lazy Days

Summer is a kind season for Glacier's beasts. Bighorn sheep rams keep together in nearly exclusive groups. A sheep study in Glacier, being done by United States Geologic Survey researcher Kim Keating, indicates that rams and ewes don't share much habitat in the summer. They stay separate until the fall breeding season.

Diving for a Dinner

A bull moose comes up after plunging its head into a lake bottom looking for a meal in August, 1992. Moose are fairly common in Glacier, though it's amazing how an animal that weighs more than 1,000 pounds can disappear into the brush with just two steps. Moose have long legs which help them not only wade in lakes, but also wade through snow in the winter. They have a reputation for being as ornery as a grizzly. This photo was taken from a safe distance with a long telephoto lens.

The white-tailed ptarmigan is one of Glacier's chameleons. It turns all white in the winter and becomes a mottled brownish white in the summer. They're extremely difficult to spot, but once you do, they aren't camera shy.

Summertime is velvet time for North Fork whitetails. They become far more wary by fall.

A Hiker's Paradise

Glacier offers get rewards for those willing to do a little hiking. There is no better place than Glacier's backcountry, particularly on a pleasant summer day, like this shot taken in the summer of 1991. A hiking staff is always a good companion. It comes in very handy when going downhill. The downhill can be tougher than the up.

Spring Fling

Early spring is a good time to see black bears in Glacier. A generally shy creature, black bears can be difficult to photograph because they are most active at dusk and dawn. But in this shot, the light is perfect.

Chris Peterson and Tom Ulrich

Over the past eight years, photography at the Hungry Horse News has seen significant changes. Many of the photos taken on a day-to-day basis are now shot with a digital 35 mm Nikon camera, that quite frankly, is built like a tank.

The use of digital cameras has streamlined production, is more environmentally friendly and you can take a picture and have it on the press in a matter of minutes. More than once during the fires of 2003 the entire front page of the newspaper was torn down and rebuilt using digital images taken from the night before deadline.

No "souping" film. No making prints.

Having said that, there is still something special about film. Many of these favorites and final edits were taken with a trusty old Leica M6 — a lightweight rangefinder camera that uses legendary Leica glass. A Nikon with long telephoto lenses was used to take much of the wildlife.

The film has advanced as well — a 35 mm slide can be enlarged significantly with virtually no grain.

Barely awake from a long winter nap, a black bear looks out from its den high in an old dead cottonwood, April, 2005.

The problem today is this: What camera to use? More often than not, I take everything, just in case, because if I leave something behind, I wish I had it.

I use the Leica for scenics and close-ups, a Nikon F5 for film work with telephoto lenses and the Nikon digital, which has the advantage of being versatile in low light situations and, because the charged coupled device that records the image is smaller than film, the magnification is greater.

Some of the grizzly bear photos taken in this section wouldn't be possible without the use of a digital camera — the bear was too far away or the light was failing.

In this section we also include photos taken by friend Tom Ulrich, who, through the years, has provided the Hungry Horse News with many memorable images.

Digital or film, the process of making photos is still the same. Load up the pack, head for the hills and see what God will give you.

There is no better life. No greater place. No finer feeling than a day well spent in Glacier National Park.

— *Chris Peterson*

Rebuilt and restored by the Ford Motor Company, the red buses returned to Glacier on June 8, 2002. The plan was to offer tours in the new reds on the east side of the park, along with a huge party at East Glacier Lodge. Mother Nature, however, dumped about three feet of snow. Glacier Park Inc., which owned the fleet, donated the buses to the the National Parks Foundation, which, in turn, gave them to the National Park Service. The restored buses retained the original shell, but were built on new chassis and with better engines. Here, Michael Levine swipes the snow off of bus 112. They had to keep the snow off of them to keep the canvas tops from collapsing.

The Wedding Tree

The rain had driven me from my fishing along the North Fork of the Flathead and I was walking out of the woods when a double rainbow appeared over the wedding tree, so named because folks occasionally get married there. I ran as fast as I could to the tree and took this photo before the light faded. The tree is one of the oldest junipers in the Park.

With its tremendous abundance of wildflowers, Glacier is naturally home to hummingbirds. This one feeds its young at the Fish Creek amphitheater.

Soaked, a cinannon black bear looks a lot like a grizzly, notice the long snout and ears however — trademarks of a black bear, not a griz. Photo was taken in the summer of 2004 as bear munched berries to the delight of spectators along the road.

Tom Ulrich photo

Bathed in autumn light, a grizzly bear digs up voles at Logan Pass. Bears feed voraciously just before they den.

Rocky Point

A favorite winter ski excursion is out to Rocky Point along Lake McDonald. Here, Danny Lewis takes in the view in the winter of 2003. Winter can be a tough time to photograph Glacier's west side. It is often cloudy and damp. It usually takes an arctic high pressure system to clear skies and with that come temperatures of 30 below or less.

Pine martens are curious creatures. They run away at first and then almost always look back. Notice the notch out of his ear, he must have escaped an enemy of some sor. This photo was taken in the fall of 2004 in the Robert Fire burned area. There was one patch of green in a sea of black trees, which suited this guy just fine. Martens generally live in heavy forests and aren't seen.

The long-tailed weasel is a cousin to the pine marten. Both are effective predators. Here, one peers from the pre-dawn grass at Logan Pass.

I was just about to leave the Many Glacier Valley in October of 2001 after spending the day photographing bighorn sheep on Mount Henkel. The sheep weren't very cooperative and I thought the day was a bust. As I drove down the road I glanced in my rear view mirror and this grizzly was standing there. It went back into the brush a few feet and out of sight. I knew it was trying to cross the road so I just waited and sure enough, just a few yards ahead of me, the bear popped out into the October evening light. I managed to take exactly two photos with a 400 mm lens before the bear dashed off, swam Swiftcurrent Creek and was off toward Mount Allen.

The fires of 2003 blackened more than 130,000 acres in Glacier National Park. The regeneration in 2004, however, sprung back quickly, drawing bears to the lush new growth. While this black bear cub may look a little sad, he was just following his mother through a black patch to greener pastures.

Robert Runs

On August 10, 2003, the Robert Fire made a spectacular run down to Lake McDonald after jumping the Camas and Inside North Fork Roads. Stoked by high winds, the fire burned right to the edge of the lake. This is a timed exposure — about three minutes, using a telephoto lens. The day was Sunday and none of the other journalists were working. All the photos on that historic day were exclusives. Shot at night, wildfires take on a surreal quality. I shot the rest of the fire season at night that year.

117

Painting with the Light

That same night the flames overtook Rocky Point. Amazingly, many of the large ponderosa pines survived, while the lodgepole pines were obliterated. Fire was once viewed as a menace in Glacier. Now it is often viewed as a natural process, provided it wasn't started by human means. The Robert Fire started outside the Park north of Columbia Falls near an old campfire. Because of this and because of its threat to buildings and structures, the federal government tried to put it out. The fire was eventually halted by intentionally burning out trees ahead of it along the face of Mount Stanton. The burned out forest then either slows or stops the main fire. The strategy worked. The fire did not go further up the McDonald Valley. A similar 'burnout' strategy was used on Apgar Mountain, where the blaze was stopped from threatening West Glacier. As a photographer, I viewed it with awe. This was light of historic consequences.

July 23, 2004, the Trapper Fire burned up and over the Sun Highway. A lightning-caused fire, it was allowed to burn until it reached the highway. I was working several different cameras as the flames roared to the roadside. This shot was on the end of a roll I forgot about. Months later, I had the film developed. I have no idea who the girl is, but she looks concerned in this frame. In others, she is laughing. Folks stayed so long to watch the flames, they had to run to their cars to escape.

While working on some photos of Coal Creek, just outside Glacier in the North Fork, I heard this little 'whump,' and noticed a pygmy owl had killed a vole. The owls, which are no large than a fist, call the dense forests of Glacier home.

121

Fall Snack

A moose munches on autumn-tinged leaves in Many Glacier, the fall of 2004. Above: A moose strolls down the Inside North Fork Road, autumn, 1999.

Stick close, while I keep watch. Mama marmot and youngster, near Cracker Lake.

I lugged all my camping gear and food plus two camera bodies and a 400mm lens up Boulder Pass in September 2002. I took this photo and many others, of pikas gathering grass in the talus slopes below the toilet. In fact, I was sitting on the throne when I spotted the pikas. The bathroom is primitive by any standard. No walls. No roof. Just a box. The pikas put on a show. They don't hibernate in winter. They build up big mats of grass in their dens to make it through Glacier's long, cold, season.

Glacier's Gardens

Balsam root sprout from the Park's east side prairies in a dazzling display of color. They become wind-whipped, however, and the petals don't last long.

If the rains come just right, Many Glacier will spring into color.

A mule deer buck partakes of paintbrush in Preston Park, summer, 2004.

Fireweed

A mountain goat will eat almost anything, including fireweed. The native plant is common in avalanche slopes. It gets its name not from its purple flower, but from the bright fiery red the leaves and stem turn as the plant begins to die. This summer of 2003 photo was never published.

Right: Finding a sunny spot, this grizzly bear takes a break. These photos were taken from the safety of a vehicle. Never approach or feed a bear. Ten people have died in Glacier from grizzly bear attacks and many more have been mauled and bitten.

In 2001, the Moose fire swept through the North Fork region of the park, mowing down lodgepole pine like matchsticks. By the spring of 2004, lush grasses and other forb had sprouted, attracting bears like this beautiful grizzly, which spent the better part of the evening feeding and lounging around.

Even in what seem like the most desolate places, life persists in fantastic fashion in Glacier. Summer, 2004.

In November of 2003 I rode my bike up the Sun Road toward Dead Horse Point. The highway was closed to vehicles, so I had the road to myself. On a ridge stood this ram. It was breeding season and he was courting several ewes. He must have survived a terrible fall at some point in his life — his right horn was completely broken off. have never seen him again.

...he reflection of the sunset on the mountains is called alpenglow. It was particularly pleasant in this March, 2004 evening. You'll see this sort of light in the winter once, maybe ...ice, if you're lucky.

Tom Ulrich pho

A mountain goat relaxes at Logan Pass.

It's a big world out there. This little black bear was busy eating berries in Many Glacier. He poked his head out just long enough to take this photo, with a 400 mm lens.

Going-to-the-Sun

A fleeting rainbow shoots up the flank of Going-to-the-Sun Mountain on a cold day in the late summer of 2004.

Bear grass at dawn. Mount Reynolds is in the background. Bear grass blooms are cyclical in nature, which helps ensure the plant's overall survival.

A white-tailed ptarmigan makes its way down Logan Pass on the first day the Sun Road was open in 2004. In the background is Mount Reynolds

In the Evening

On a hot summer day as the sun went down, this mountain goat grabbed a windy ledge to cool off and get away from the flies. Goats are hounded by biting flies in the summertime.

A back bear stands up to get a better look around while feeding in Glacier, April, 2004.

One of the rarer owls in Glacier is the great gray. I got lucky. This one flew in front of my truck on the Park's Inside North Fork Road and then sat in a branch while I took its photo. Great grays are normally nocturnal and very shy.

As the sun goes down and mom keeps eating, this black bear cub decides to stay close. This photo has never been published, taken in April, 2004.

About halfway through a backcountry ski excursison from Polebridge to Apgar, in March, 2004, I came upon this moose antler. The rest of the moose is under the snow — ~~s~~eriously, it was a shed. Notice the wear on the ends.

Cold, Windy

The wind was howling when I took this early spring photo of Two Medicine Lake. The road into the lake is usually one of the first to open on the east side. It is a rare day when the wind isn't blowing here. Two Medicine is one of the most rugged regions of the park. As such, it sees fewer visitors.

One of the first bear photos I ever took for the Hungry Horse News was this cub on a log near Lake McDonald Lodge in 1999. I've driven by the same spot thousands of times and have never seen a bear there again. I suspect this little guy may have had a mother nearby, but I never saw her if it did. It wasn't any bigger than a small dog.

One of the greatest thrills of 2004 was to capture a wolverine in Glacier. Gulo gulo is an elusive beast. This one walked right in front of me. It was feeding on a dead goat at the foot of Piegan Mountain in November.

October sunset, Logan Pass.

cloud nine after climbing to the summit of Mount Siyeh was Chris Hanson in August, 1999. Normally the view from Siyeh's sheer north face looks some 3,500 vertical feet
n at Cracker Lake. On this day, we went up through the clouds. Just before the summit we broke through them. Being above the clouds was far more interesting.

Until we meet again.